HOW TO BE EXTRA-ORDINARY

Real-life stories of extraordinary humans!

written by
Rashmi Sirdeshpande

illustrated by
Annabel Tempest

PUFFIN

SIR DAVID ATTENBOROUGH
A naturalist who brought the whole world into our homes

Ever since he was a little boy, David was always fascinated by nature. Born in England in 1926, he had quite a collection of fossils and would disappear for weeks looking for new ones. He was given a salamander at 8, which started his lifelong animal family: from chameleons, pythons, hummingbirds, and gibbons to lemurs, chimpanzees, and bush babies!

When David joined the British Broadcasting Corporation (the BBC) in 1952, like most people at the time, he didn't have a TV and had only ever seen one TV show. But still . . .

He made some AMAZING documentaries.
Life on Earth (1979) had over 500 million viewers. BBC's Wildlife on One ran for 28 years from 1977–2005. Planet Earth (2006) was the biggest wildlife documentary EVER.

He changed the face of television.
David produced the Zoo Quest series, which – for the first time – filmed animals in the wild and in zoos, rather than in the studio. At first, he was kept off the screen (because his boss thought his teeth were too big!) but when the presenter dropped out, David stepped in . . . and he was a natural.

He's one of the most travelled human beings in history (if you don't count astronauts)!
He travelled 256,000 miles for his *The Life of Birds* documentary.
That's like travelling around the world – **10 TIMES**.

He's been bitten by a python, charged by a rhino, and cuddled by mountain gorillas!

Always keep a respectful distance . . .

THE PEOPLE HAVE VOTED!

2018 UK poll
The most trustworthy public figure

2018 UK poll
Ultimate dream neighbour

He's woken up the world to many important issues like climate change and plastic pollution. His documentary *Blue Planet II* (2017) inspired people all over the globe to reduce their use of plastics after showing how much harm they cause – Queen Elizabeth was also inspired!

No more plastic straws or bottles at Buckingham Palace!

"The future of humanity, and, indeed, all life on Earth, now depends on us."

Real name: KRYSTYNA SKARBEK

Code name: Christine Granville (or "Pauline", or "Willing")

Special skill: Getting out of sticky situations

Born in Poland in 1908, Krystyna Skarbek was Britain's first female spy. As a child, she loved horse riding, hiking, and skiing. When the Second World War began, she sailed from Cape Town to Southampton and demanded a job with the British secret service. They weren't too sure about having a female spy, but Krystyna – and her sporty talents – were going to come in handy . . .

OPERATION BARBAROSSA

Once, Krystyna skied out of Poland with early film evidence of Nazi plans to invade Soviet Russia hidden inside her gloves!

In 1941, when she was caught by the Gestapo (the Nazi secret police), she managed to get herself and her friend released with her quick thinking. Krystyna pretended they had tuberculosis, a terrible – and very contagious – illness. The prison hospital chest X-ray showed that her lungs were horribly scarred, so the Gestapo released them.

COUGH, COUGH! You really don't want to catch this!

PSST! My lungs were **actually** scarred because of my old office job at a car dealership. All those yucky fumes!

Krystyna was also fluent in French, and so in 1944 she was parachuted into occupied France, where she rescued 3 agents. She cycled 25 miles to the Nazi-controlled prison, despite being terrified of cycling. She hummed a tune to find out which cells the agents were in – and they hummed it back! She then persuaded the guards to let the prisoners go.

Bonjour!

Krystyna was once caught holding a top-secret silk map. She wasn't scared – she just smiled at the German officers and rolled it into a headscarf.

Krystyna was awarded the OBE (Order of the British Empire), the George Medal, and the French Croix de Guerre for her services.

These are just a few of Krystyna's many courageous missions. Sadly, for all her bravery, she didn't get the recognition she deserved in her lifetime. Once the war was over, Krystyna had to fight to become a citizen of Britain. The secret service didn't want to give her a permanent job, despite her many talents.

Krystyna found work cleaning bathrooms on a cruise ship, and was later murdered in a tragic incident. She is only just starting to get the respect she deserves over 50 years after her death.

"She is no longer wanted."

"Cannot type, has no experience whatsoever of office work and is altogether not a very easy person to employ."

Aeham Ahmad
The Pianist of Yarmouk

"Music is an extraordinary peace-builder; its universal language reaches straight to the heart and brings down barriers of separation."

Aeham was born in Damascus (the Syrian capital) in 1988, and lived in Yarmouk, a Palestinian refugee camp. His father, a blind violinist, taught Aeham to play piano when he was just 5 years old. Aeham grew up to become a piano teacher with a music shop in Yarmouk.

Civil war broke out in Syria in 2011, and by early 2013 Yarmouk was under siege. This meant that food, water, and medicines were scarce. Aeham wanted to lift the community's spirits and give them a vision of a happier, more peaceful time. And he wanted the world to see that Syrian civilians were trying to survive and stay hopeful. But how?

I wanted to give the children hope. They had no food, no school to go to.

So Aeham put his old piano on a wagon and, with the help of his friends and students, pushed it out into the streets. He then risked his life to play music and sing in the rubble – and his friends uploaded videos to YouTube for the world to see.

"I wanted to give them a beautiful dream. To change this black colour at least into grey."

In 2015, the militant group ISIS banned music in Syria. Aeham's piano was burnt down before his eyes and his life was in danger. He became one of 600,000 refugees to make the perilous 2,400-mile journey across the Mediterranean and north through Europe. It was so dangerous that his wife and toddlers had to stay in Syria. This broke Aeham's heart.

Our doors are open.

Angela Merkel
Chancellor of Germany

Aeham reached Munich, Germany, in 2015 and found a home in Wiesbaden. He performed over 250 concerts across Europe to share his message of unity and hope, and his memories of Syria.

Aeham was always determined to play the music he loved. His hand was injured in Syria so he couldn't play like he used to. But he didn't stop.

THE PIANIST FROM YARMOUK
AEHAM AHMAD

He was finally granted asylum in Germany in May 2016 and was soon joined by his wife and children. After their happy reunion, he stayed up into the night, playing with his children and talking to his wife. He woke up at 6 a.m. the next morning . . . and went straight to perform in his next concert!

KEIKO FUKUDA SENSEI
Grandmaster Judoka

Born in Tokyo in 1913, Keiko Fukuda was less than 5 feet tall but, aged 98, she became the only woman in the world to be awarded the 10th dan – the highest rank – in judo. Martial arts were in her blood. Her grandfather was a jujitsu master, and her grandmother came from a samurai warrior family. Keiko was the last living student of the creator of judo, Jigoro Kano Sensei.

"Judo" means *the gentle way* – using SKILL and FLEXIBILITY to beat STRENGTH. It might sound easy but it's really hard. You have to use just the right amount of strength – *it*'s not about hurting your opponent, it's more about self-control and respect. Students meditate, and at the start of each practice they bow to their mat, to their teachers, and to each other.

When she was 21, Keiko joined the women's division of the Kodokan, Kano Sensei's dojo. Her mother and grandmother had trained her for marriage, teaching her things like flower arranging and the art of the Japanese tea ceremony. But the only training Keiko was interested in was judo. In those days, women had to choose – marriage or work, marriage or judo. Keiko chose judo.

She practised for 3 hours a day, 6 days a week. During the Second World War, she braved the streets of Tokyo to travel to the Kodokan every day, walking past burning houses and risking her life in the air raids.

After the war was over, Keiko was invited to California to teach judo. Kano Sensei had told his students to spread judo all over the world and this was her chance.

Be strong, be gentle, be beautiful.

In 1966, Keiko moved to San Francisco, where she eventually set up her own women's dojo, the Soko Joshi Judo Club. She taught there for over 40 years, showing women and girls that they could practise judo – no matter their age or size.

Even though Keiko was one of the greatest judo teachers in the world, she struggled to gain recognition for her skill. The Kodokan in Tokyo, the global judo HQ, wouldn't let women achieve more than the 5th dan. Keiko was awarded 5th dan in 1953 but stayed at that level for almost 20 YEARS until her student Shelley Fernandez convinced the Kodokan to award her the 6th dan in 1972.

It wasn't until 2011, when she was 98, that USA Judo promoted her to 10th dan, the highest rank possible in judo. At the time she was one of only 4 living people to hold that honour, and she continued teaching judo until just before her death in 2013 at the age of 99.

Nelson Mandela
Freedom Fighter. Father of a Nation.

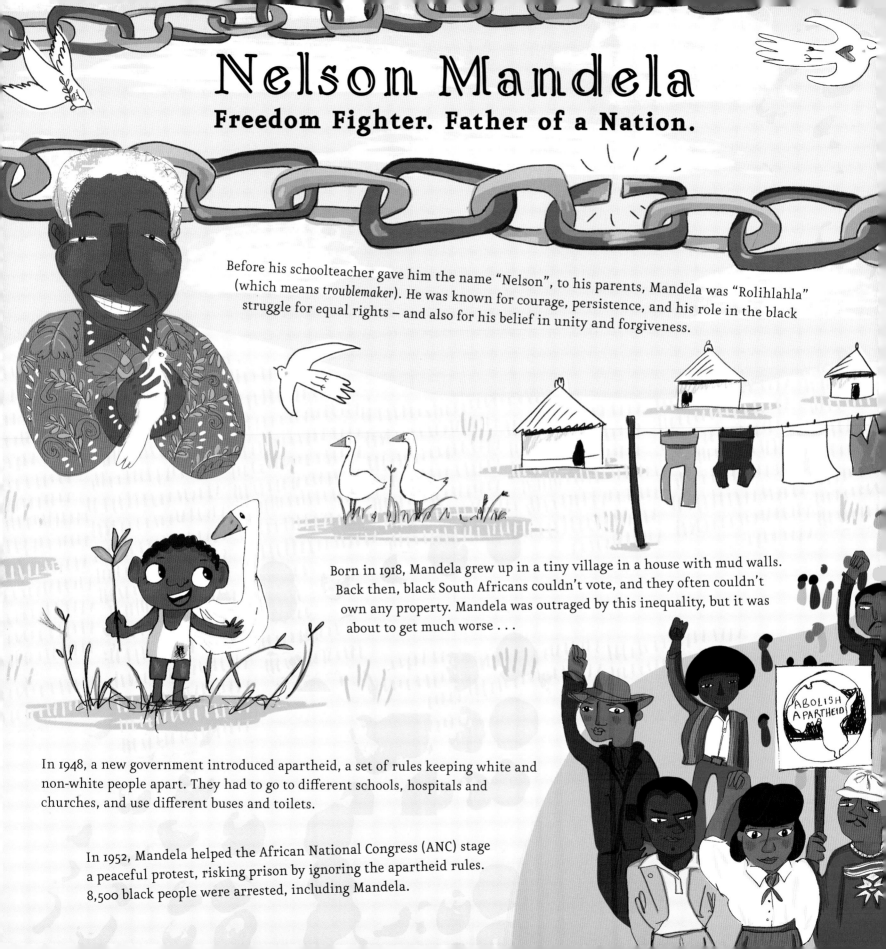

Before his schoolteacher gave him the name "Nelson", to his parents, Mandela was "Rolihlahla" (which means *troublemaker*). He was known for courage, persistence, and his role in the black struggle for equal rights – and also for his belief in unity and forgiveness.

Born in 1918, Mandela grew up in a tiny village in a house with mud walls. Back then, black South Africans couldn't vote, and they often couldn't own any property. Mandela was outraged by this inequality, but it was about to get much worse . . .

In 1948, a new government introduced apartheid, a set of rules keeping white and non-white people apart. They had to go to different schools, hospitals and churches, and use different buses and toilets.

In 1952, Mandela helped the African National Congress (ANC) stage a peaceful protest, risking prison by ignoring the apartheid rules. 8,500 black people were arrested, including Mandela.

ABOLISH APARTHEID

Over the next 10 years, Mandela was repeatedly in trouble with the law but he never stopped campaigning for change – and the authorities were determined to silence him. Eventually, in 1962, he was arrested, and in 1964 he was sentenced to life imprisonment.

"I have cherished the ideal of a democratic and free society in which all persons live together in harmony and with equal opportunities."

Mandela was 46 when he was sentenced. He was only allowed one visitor a year and one letter every 6 months (even then, much of it would be scribbled out). He was 71 when he was released in February 1990 – that's 27 long years behind bars.

46664

But he still had work to do! In 1991, he became leader of the ANC and worked with President F.W. de Klerk to end apartheid and make sure black South Africans got the vote. In 1993, they were awarded the Nobel Peace Prize, and in April 1994 Mandela was voted President.

When a deep injury is done to us, we never heal until we forgive.

Mandela shocked people with his ability to forgive and make peace with his oppressors. He let white officials who had worked under apartheid keep their positions in government. He even invited an old jailer to his inauguration dinner.

"No one is born hating another person because of the colour of his skin, or his background, or his religion."

Mandela's vision of South Africa wasn't just about fighting for the rights of black people. It was about freedom and equality for EVERYONE, regardless of their colour.

DR SAU LAN WU
Particle Physicist – studying the building blocks of the universe

Sau Lan was born in Japanese-occupied Hong Kong during the Second World War. She grew up in severe poverty, sleeping in the corridor of a rice shop. Her mother was illiterate but did everything she could to make sure Sau Lan had a good education.

If you persist, something good is bound to happen.

Sau Lan dreamed of being a painter, but after reading a biography of scientist Marie Curie, she was inspired to follow in her footsteps.

Against the wishes of her father, Sau Lan secretly applied to 50 colleges in the USA and got a scholarship to study Physics at Vassar College. When she sailed to the USA in 1960, she had just $40 to her name – even her clothes were donated by local students. There weren't many female physicists in the 1970s and 80s, and Sau Lan felt she always had to work harder to prove herself. Now she's a world-famous particle physicist.

A CRASH COURSE IN PARTICLE PHYSICS
The universe is made up of atoms.
Atoms are made up of electrons, protons and neutrons.
Protons and neutrons break down into even TINIER particles called quarks. Particle physics (or high energy physics) is the study of these tiny particles and how they work.

Sau Lan had a personal goal to make at least 3 major discoveries. And she did!

1974: She helped discover the CHARM QUARK, a very basic level of matter. This was a real surprise and it changed how scientists think about matter.

1979: Her calculations were key in the discovery of the GLUON, the glue that holds quarks together.

2012: She was an important part of the team that found a particle that looks like the HIGGS BOSON. It's also called the God Particle because without it, there would be no atoms, no humans, and no galaxies! Sau Lan spent 30 years of experiment after experiment looking for this particle. It's a sneaky one!

It's like looking for a needle in a haystack the size of a football stadium!

WOW

DARK MATTER

The Higgs boson was observed at the Large Hadron Collider (LHC) at CERN, Geneva. It's the biggest machine in the world (17 miles long!). It's used to crash particles together to break them open and see what's inside!

Now, Sau Lan is looking for the particles that make up DARK MATTER, an invisible substance that accounts for a big chunk (about one quarter) of the universe.

"It's out there in the galaxies, but we don't see it here on Earth. Still, I'm going to try."

I focus everything on the finish line. "Keep going," I tell myself. "Keep going."

Mo was born in Somalia in 1983 and moved to Britain when he was 8 years old. He hardly spoke any English so school was tough. He was also cheeky and full of energy, often getting into trouble. He dreamed of being a footballer, but it was his running that caught the eye of his PE teacher, Alan Watkinson, when Mo was 11. Alan took him under his wing and (using a football kit as a bribe!) set him on a path to become a double Olympic champion.

Mo's first break came aged 13, when he won the English Schools' cross country race, and, aged 18, he won his first European Juniors 5,000m gold medal. Mo ran a lot and he ran well – but something was missing. Then he moved in with some Kenyan athletes, who were 100% dedicated to running. They trained hard, ate well, studied races, and went to bed early. If Mo wanted to be the best distance runner, he had to focus everything on his sport. And he did.

Twice DOUBLE Olympic Champion (10,000m and 5,000m in 2012 and 2016)

3 World Championship gold medals (10,000m)

3 World Championship gold medals (5,000m)

6 European Championship wins

5 Great North Run wins

Mo's training regime is intense. He runs 126 to 135 miles a week, and sometimes trains on an underwater treadmill. He spends 6 months every year training at high altitude in Arizona, Ethiopia or the French Pyrenees. He misses his wife and 4 children, but he has to keep his eye on his goal.

Mo is now focusing on marathons. The switch hasn't been easy. Mo finished 8th in his first London Marathon in 2014 but shook it off and carried on training – he knows that, sometimes, you don't reach your goal.

I tried my hardest and gave 110% – that's all you can do.

FARAH

Mo is all about taking on a challenge, training harder, and getting better. In 2018, he went on to finish 3rd in the London Marathon, and then won the Chicago Marathon just 6 months later! In the future, he wants to work with children to build the next generation of British athletes.

"Keep climbing that ladder, but . . . Don't lose sight of the fun."

Judith Kerr
Author-Illustrator. Refugee.

"If you've got a life that so many people didn't have, you can't waste it."

Led by Adolf Hitler, the Nazi Party came to power in Germany in 1933 and would rule until 1945. The Nazis had many extreme beliefs, and, among others, Jewish people (like Judith's family) were in particular danger. Judith's father, Alfred Kerr, was a theatre critic and writer who spoke out against the Nazis. They later burned his books and put a price on his head.

In February 1933, when Judith was 9 years old, Alfred got a tip-off that saved their lives. He was warned by a policeman that his home would be raided and his passport confiscated, so he fled to Zurich, Switzerland, and waited for his family to join him.

Judith later wrote a trilogy about their escape from Nazi Germany. The first book was called *When Hitler Stole Pink Rabbit*.

On 4 March 1933, Judith escaped Berlin late at night on the milk train with her mother and her brother. As they approached the Swiss border, her mother told her not to say ANYTHING. When the officers let them pass, Judith almost blurted out, "There you are, nothing's happened!" Her mother gave her a stern look so she kept quiet. Two days later their home in Berlin was raided and their possessions were seized.

Alfred struggled to get work in Zurich and the family moved to Paris before settling in London in March 1936. But then, in September 1939, Britain and France declared war on Germany. With its food shortages and bombing raids, the Second World War affected civilians more than previous wars.

Judith had always loved drawing and after the war she went to art school in London. Judith went on to create some of the world's best-loved picture books, notably *The Tiger Who Came to Tea* and the Mog series, inspired by a collection of her cats. She has published over 30 books, and together they've sold more than 10 million copies and have been translated into over 20 languages.

I can never forget how lucky I've been.

Judith is a creature of habit. She created all her books at the same drawing table in the same attic in her house in London. (Her kitchen cupboards haven't changed since she illustrated them in *The Tiger Who Came to Tea*!) It's over 50 years since her first book and she still draws almost every day. Thanks to the bravery of her parents, and their lucky escape, Judith has been able to create some of the best-loved books, read by children all around the world.

PROFESSOR STEPHEN HAWKING
Theoretical Physicist. Cosmologist.

"My goal is simple. It is a complete understanding of the universe, why it is as it is and why it exists at all."

Stephen was born on 8 January 1942, exactly 300 years after the death of the famous astronomer Galileo. One of the most influential scientists of the 20th century, Stephen dedicated his whole life to understanding where the universe came from.

At the age of 21, while studying cosmology at Cambridge University, Stephen was diagnosed with motor neurone disease (which affects the nerves). His doctors said he had 2 years to live, but he survived for another 55! The diagnosis made him work even harder to uncover the secrets of the universe in the time he had left, and to work around his condition.

Galileo (1564–1642)

Stephen was a theoretical physicist. This means he used HYPOTHESES – educated guesses – and complicated maths to figure out how the universe works. And, like all good scientists, he wasn't afraid to admit his mistakes and start again.

His amazing work helped us to understand black holes. At first, scientists thought they had such a strong pull that nothing could escape them, not even light. But Stephen showed that little bursts of energy could escape.

"Because every new day could be my last, I have developed a desire to make the most of each and every minute."

BANG

Stephen applied his black hole maths to the Big Bang theory, and showed how our universe came into being 13 billion years ago from a small and infinitely dense point in space–time (a singularity), which rapidly expanded into stars and galaxies! To prove this, Stephen combined two opposing theories in physics:

Einstein's Theory of Relativity (how gravity affects HUGE objects like stars and planets)
and
Quantum Mechanics (the behaviour of the TINIEST particles of matter)

Stephen wanted his knowledge to be available to everyone, not just physicists. So he wrote a number of books that explained the origins of the universe in more simple terms.

Stephen always said he was very lucky to have the support of his family, nurses and doctors, and the fantastic technology that helped him continue his work. He married twice, had 3 children, travelled the world, and even experienced zero gravity when training for space travel! Stephen died on 14 March 2018 – he never made it into space, but after his death a recording of his words was beamed over to the nearest black hole.

"I have spent my life travelling across the universe inside my mind. Through theoretical physics, I have sought to answer some of the great questions but there are other challenges, other big questions which must be answered . . ."

Wangari Maathai
Environmental Activist. Changemaker.

> It's the little things citizens do. That's what will make the difference. My little thing is planting trees.

Known to Kenyans as "Mama Miti" (*mother of trees*), Wangari was born in a rural village in the highlands of Kenya in 1940. When Wangari was growing up, the forest was thick and full of animals, and the water was clean. The soil was fertile and people could grow their own crops. Over the years, the forest was cut down and the soil overworked because of commercial farming. The streams were polluted and the local communities were getting poorer and poorer. Something had to be done.

On World Environment Day in 1977, Wangari and a small group of women planted 7 trees in Nairobi to mark the first Green Belt. People laughed at first, but the villagers taught other villagers how to plant trees. Slowly, Wangari's Green Belt Movement spread from village to village . . .

country to country . . .

and it grew . . .

from a tiny seed of an idea into something BIG.

Over 50 million trees have been planted so far and the movement has expanded across a number of African countries. It has provided jobs and education for hundreds of thousands of rural women, teaching them how to plant trees for food and fuel, grow crops, and set up gardens to feed their families.

Wangari saw a clear link between Kenya's poverty and environmental problems, and the corrupt government. She spoke out against the dictator, President Moi, and even fought his plans to build a 62-storey skyscraper in one of Nairobi's green spaces (she won!). Moi targeted Wangari and she was arrested many times and intimidated. But she didn't stop fighting for the protection of the environment and a corruption-free government.

People often ask me what drives me. Perhaps the more difficult question would be: What would it take to stop me?

In 2004, Wangari was awarded the Nobel Peace Prize for her work to promote environmental conservation, women's rights, and democracy. She was the first African woman to be given this award.

Wangari died in 2011 aged 71, but her legacy lives on. She inspired the Billion Tree Campaign led by the United Nations, which has planted more than 15 billion trees in over 190 countries across the world. And it all began with 7 little seeds planted in Nairobi all those years ago!

DAVID NOTT
War Surgeon. Humanitarian.

Born in Wales in 1956, David struggled at school but still managed to become one of the UK's top consultant surgeons. For over 25 years, David has taken several months of unpaid leave each year to volunteer in some of the most dangerous conflict and natural disaster zones all over the world. He's been everywhere from Afghanistan, Syria, and Iraq to Sierra Leone, Haiti, and Nepal, training local doctors and saving countless lives.

Life is so precious . . . and to try and preserve it is a wonderful thing.

Shortly after becoming a surgeon, David saw footage of the war in Sarajevo, Bosnia. Watching the suffering there, he knew he had to do something. So he flew to Sarajevo and volunteered in the "Swiss Cheese Hospital" (it was called that because it was so full of holes from bombing raids!).

"It is very difficult — there's no doubt — but when you can see you make a very real difference, you simply cannot turn your back."

During a blast, the whole room would shake while he operated. The lights would suddenly go off and someone would have to come in with a lamp.

Despite the huge danger, David kept going back to war zones and working with local doctors in makeshift hospitals with very basic equipment. The hospitals were sometimes in tents or underground, with the sound of bombs and gunfire coming from just outside. David didn't take sides when it came to saving lives – he would operate on anyone.

"We're all human beings."

Once, in Gaza in 2014, David was operating on a 7-year-old girl. Suddenly, they heard that the hospital was about to be blown up. Everyone left except David and his anaesthetist. They just couldn't leave the little girl like that. Fortunately, nothing happened and David lived to carry on his good work. But experiences like these took their toll on him, and it took him a long time to recover from the trauma of each visit.

In 2015, David set up the David Nott Foundation with his wife, Elly. This foundation trains doctors from around the world to work in areas of war and natural disaster. David still feels he should be on the front line, but now he has a family of his own he is focusing, for the time being, on training more people like him.

"It's the legacy I am trying to leave. To be a war surgeon is a fine art, knowing the right thing to do for a patient with what's available."

Michelle Obama

Activist. Mother. Lawyer.
Former First Lady of the United States.

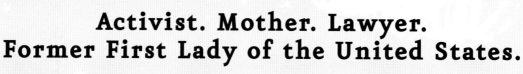

White House Code Name: **Renaissance**
(former President Barack Obama's
was "**Renegade**")

Renaissance is on
the move!

"There is no magic to achievement. It's really about hard work, choices and persistence."

Born in 1964, Michelle grew up in the South Side of Chicago, USA. Even though neither of her parents went to college, she graduated from Princeton and Harvard, and worked hard to become a successful city lawyer. When her husband, Barack Obama, was elected President of the United States, Michelle became the first African-American First Lady.

Traditionally, the First Lady is the White House hostess. First Lady Eleanor Roosevelt (1933–1945) expanded this role and Michelle Obama put her own stamp on it too. Michelle was a hostess but also an activist and someone people could connect with.

She got her hands dirty!
In 2009, she invited local schoolchildren to help her dig up the White House lawn! They built the White House Kitchen Garden, which started a national conversation about being healthy. It also inspired families and communities all over the USA to grow their own vegetables. The garden has over 50 types of fruits, vegetables, and herbs!

Her big dream is to educate 62 MILLION girls around the world.
Millions of girls aren't in school for many different reasons, such as poverty, war, cultural issues, and a lack of schools. Michelle's Let Girls Learn campaign pledged $1 billion to over 50 countries to provide scholarships, safe transport, and encourage local governments to make a change.

> I'll be fighting for girls' education for the rest of my life.

This is for my girls!

She encouraged people to stand up to bullies with grace.
Michelle knows what it feels like to be bullied. She was called all kinds of names as First Lady. It knocked her at first but she decided: "When someone is cruel or acts like a bully, you don't stoop to their level. No, our motto is, when they go low, we go high."

She isn't afraid to just be herself!
Michelle did a dance-off with Big Bird from *Sesame Street*. She also rocked out to Stevie Wonder and rapped with Missy Elliott in James Corden's Carpool Karaoke show.

And, despite being SO famous, she always puts family first. She has two daughters, Sasha and Malia, and says her most important title is still "Mom-in-chief".

Michelle Obama may not be in the White House any more, but she's still inspiring people!

"There are still many causes worth sacrificing for; so much history yet to be made."

Born in 1912, Alan was always obsessed with maths and science. He loved to experiment, mixing chemicals and figuring out mathematical problems. For Alan, science wasn't about learning facts – it was about thinking things through. His teachers weren't convinced by his "vague ideas", but he ended up making an incredible contribution to modern science.

Cracking the Enigma

In September 1939, the Second World War began. When he was only 27, Alan started work at Bletchley Park, where the country's top codebreakers worked – day and night – to crack the German Enigma machine. Enigma scrambled secret military messages so that only German troops with their own machine could read them. There were *billions* of possible settings, which meant that it was nearly impossible to crack the code. And the settings were changed every day at midnight, meaning that there was a different code to crack each day!

If we don't crack this by midnight, all our work is worthless and we're back to square one!

Ⓔ Ⓝ Ⓘ Ⓖ Ⓜ Ⓐ

Alan realized that only a machine could beat Enigma, and so he set out to build one: "the Bombe". He found a weakness in the code to help him: the messages often contained predictable words like the names of military officers or weather information. Once a bit of the code was cracked, the machine could use *that* information to crack the rest. It was like solving a crossword puzzle.

Along with codebreaker Gordon Welchman, Alan perfected the Bombe until it could solve an Enigma setting within just ONE HOUR. The top-secret information it revealed saved millions of lives and shortened the Second World War by at least a few years.

Can computers **think?**

100 years earlier, Ada Lovelace said that machines could follow instructions. Alan Turing took this one step further — maybe they could think! In 1950, he devised the TURING TEST to see whether a computer could fool you into thinking that it's human. This idea of building an intelligent computer (or robot!) is a big inspiration to Artificial Intelligence (AI) developers today.

Bletchley Park

Sadly, Alan's last few years were unhappy ones. In 1952, when the police found out he was in a relationship with a man (which was illegal in Britain at that time), he was charged with "gross indecency" and banned from working for the secret service. The law has since changed and Alan was given a Royal Pardon in 2013.

Alan died of cyanide poisoning at just 41. We don't know exactly what happened, but what we do know is that Alan Turing was a brilliant mind who forever changed the way we think about computers – and whose machine saved many, many lives.

FRIDA KAHLO
Artist. Revolutionary. Icon.

"At the end of the day, we can endure much more than we think we can."

Born in Mexico City in 1907, Frida Kahlo is one of the most famous female painters of the 20th century. She is known for her bold patterns and bright colours as well as her strength, her style, and her *alegría* (joyfulness and zest for life).

When Frida was 6, she contracted polio, an illness that left her with a muscle weakness in one leg, which affected how she walked. Then, when she was 18, she nearly died in a bus accident. With serious injuries to her spine, ribs, shoulder, collarbone, and pelvis, from that day on she lived with chronic pain. The surgeons had to piece her together like a collage.

I paint self-portraits because I am so often alone, because I am the person I know best.

While she recovered, Frida turned to painting. Her mother arranged for a special easel so she could paint lying down with the help of a mirror.

Many of Frida's 200 works of art are self-portraits. They helped her make sense of her pain and frustration at a time when it wasn't okay for women to show strong feelings in public. (She also often painted her body cast when in hospital, and she was there a lot – she had 30 major surgeries in her lifetime!) She proudly wore her thick eyebrows and moustache, challenging people's ideas of what was beautiful.

Frida, like the famous painter Diego Rivera (the love of her life), was a revolutionary and her paintings were political. She was proud of her mixed heritage and combined traditional Mexican and European fashion with ancient Aztec symbols. This showed her support for the Mexican people, who were finding their own identity at a time of great political change.

Frida's health deteriorated in the late 1940s. In 1953, at the time of her very first solo exhibition in Mexico, she was in hospital. She wanted to see the exhibition so badly that she turned up in an ambulance and they carried her in on a bed!

Frida died soon after, in 1954, at the age of 47. Her last painting was one of watermelons, which are associated with the Mexican *Día de los Muertos* (Day of the Dead). Perhaps she knew that death was near. Eight days before she died, she added 3 words: "VIVA LA VIDA", which means *long live life!*

ABDUL KALAM

Teacher. Rocket Scientist.
Former President of India.

What would you like to be remembered for?

Born in 1931 in a small temple town in South India, Abdul came from humble beginnings. A boat-owner's boy, he had a paper round before school to help his family out. He got up at 4 a.m. every day and was up studying until 11 p.m. There was no electricity at home and the oil lamps only lasted from 7 p.m. to 9 p.m., but his mother kept some oil aside just for him. Abdul's hard work paid off – he went from paper boy, to rocket scientist, to president of a nation of one billion people.

Enchanted by birds, Abdul had always dreamed of flying. He was devastated when he didn't make the cut as an Indian Air Force pilot but he decided that, if he couldn't fly, he'd make things that could. When he joined the Indian space research team, his first satellite launch vehicle (SLV) test was a disaster and the SLV-3 crashed into the sea. Abdul was frustrated but he remembered how calmly his father had rebuilt his boat after a cyclone. He tried again a year later, in 1980, and the launch was a success. India had joined the space age.

Abdul then moved to the national defence team where he worked on the development of missiles. He tried to use the missile technology to benefit ordinary people too: he used the same technology to help make a low-cost coronary stent, which helped blood flow in patients with blocked arteries.

In 2002, at the age of 70, Abdul was elected President of India. He was totally different from the other politicians. When he moved to the 340-room Rashtrapati Bhavan, the president's official residence, he stayed in the most basic room. He worried whether his staff were tired or hungry. He was adored by children and always made time for them. Raised a Muslim, he loved and respected all religions, making him the perfect president for a secular nation.

In 2007, Abdul left the Rashtrapati Bhavan with just 2 small suitcases and his library of books. He spent his later years doing what he loved most: teaching the next generation of Indians. When he died in 2015, the people of India would always remember him as the "People's President".

"Dream, dream, and dream; dreams transform into thoughts, and thoughts result in action."

TM 6/9/19

For my parents, who are all kinds of extraordinary.
With special thanks to editors Anna and Emily, and designer Steph! – R.S.
For the most EXTRAORDINARY woman I know, my mummy, Scilla Tempest – A.T.

PUFFIN BOOKS

UK | USA | Canada | Ireland | Australia | India | New Zealand | South Africa

Puffin Books is part of the Penguin Random House group of companies whose
addresses can be found at global.penguinrandomhouse.com.

www.penguin.co.uk
www.puffin.co.uk
www.ladybird.co.uk

Penguin
Random House
UK

First published 2019

001

Text copyright © Rashmi Sirdeshpande, 2019
Illustrations copyright © Annabel Tempest, 2019

The moral right of the author and illustrator has been asserted

Printed in China

A CIP catalogue record for this book is available from the British Library

ISBN: 978–0–241–38540–1

All correspondence to:
Puffin Books, Penguin Random House Children's, 80 Strand, London WC2R 0RL

FSC
www.fsc.org
MIX
Paper from
responsible sources
FSC® C018179